Longman Structural Readers: Plays
Stage 2

Inspector Thackeray Arrives

Kenneth James

Illustrated by Trevor Ridley

297-

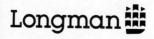

Contents

	Page
Inspector Thackeray Arrives	1
Airport Kidnap	18
The Electronic Eye	33

The three stories in this book are about Inspector Thackeray. The Inspector is a detective. A detective has a hard job. He has to find the criminal.

In these stories, the criminal makes three mistakes. The Inspector always finds those mistakes. Perhaps you will try to look for them too.

Inspector Thackeray Arrives

Characters

Inspector Thackeray
Inspector Brown
Policewoman
Fireman
Sub-officer
Mr Wood
Sergeant Silver
Peter Green
Constable

Scene 1

(*Manchester Central Police Station. Inspector Thackeray's office.*)

THACKERAY: (*answers the telephone*) Manchester Central Police Station. Detective Inspector Thackeray speaking.

BROWN: Inspector Brown here. Police School. Your new sergeant –

THACKERAY: My new sergeant. Ha! I haven't seen him yet.

BROWN: We haven't sent him yet.

THACKERAY: I know that. He's three weeks late.

BROWN: We needed him here at the school.

THACKERAY: And I needed him here at the station.

BROWN: You'll get him today. We're sending him this morning.

THACKERAY: Are you? Well this time –

BROWN: Yes, Inspector?

THACKERAY: This time I want a really good man.

BROWN: This time – you'll get a really good man. Just listen to this. There's a report in his file. I've got the file here. I'll read the report on him. He was first in English, first in Mathematics, and first in police law. Oh, and he can write a good report.

THACKERAY: I'm not asking for Einstein.

1

BROWN: You're not getting Einstein. His name's Silver. Sergeant Silver. (*The other telephone buzzes.*)

POLICEWOMAN: Information Room here. I have a message for Inspector Thackeray.

THACKERAY: Yes. Thackeray here.

POLICEWOMAN: We have a report of a large fire. The address is Johnson's Furniture Store, Piccadilly, Manchester. Johnson's Furniture Store, Piccadilly, Manchester. This message timed at 09.50 hours.

THACKERAY: Thank you, Information Room. I'll be one minute.

BROWN: Thackeray? Are you still there?

THACKERAY: Oh, it's you, Brown. You heard the message?

BROWN: Yes. I heard it. And I've read my newspaper this week, too.

THACKERAY: Your newspaper?

BROWN: That's three fires now in seven days.

THACKERAY: Four. The newspapers didn't report the third fire. It was a very small one.

BROWN: How do you know?

THACKERAY: I had to go to it.

BROWN: On police work?

THACKERAY: Yes. It was a case of arson.

BROWN: Arson! So you're looking for the man.

THACKERAY: Or the woman.

BROWN: Or the child. Young people often start fires.

THACKERAY: Yes.

BROWN: But the new sergeant. He's going to start work with you this morning. Where shall I send him?

THACKERAY: Send him to the fire. He can find me there.

Scene 2

(*Piccadilly. In front of Johnson's Furniture Store. A large fire is burning.*)

THACKERAY: Are you the leading fireman?

2

FIREMAN: I am. (*To the sub-officer*) Number two hose-line.

SUB-OFFICER: Yes, sir.

FIREMAN: I want that water on the roof. Over that third window, there. On the roof.

SUB-OFFICER: Yes, sir.

THACKERAY: Er – can you answer some questions?

FIREMAN: I can't talk now.

THACKERAY: Detective Inspector Thackeray.

FIREMAN: Be quick, Inspector.

THACKERAY: Where did the fire start?

FIREMAN: The fourth floor.

THACKERAY: I'm sorry. The noise is very bad. I didn't hear you.

FIREMAN: The fourth floor.

THACKERAY: Are there any people still in the building?

FIREMAN: Three. My men are looking for them.

THACKERAY: Ah, yes. I can see one of them now. At that window there –

FIREMAN: They've got a woman.

THACKERAY: And now there's a man – and a boy.

FIREMAN: We'll have them on the ground in a minute.

THACKERAY: I'll want to question them.

FIREMAN: They'll go to the hospital first, Inspector.

THACKERAY: I'll only be a minute.

FIREMAN: They need a doctor now. Not a policeman. They must go to the hospital.

Scene 3

(*Inspector Thackeray knocks at the door of a room in the hospital.*)

WOOD: Come in.

THACKERAY: (*goes into the room*) It's Mr Wood, isn't it?

WOOD: That's right.

THACKERAY: The hospital gave me your name.

WOOD: Perhaps the hospital can give me my clothes. I don't want to stay in this bed all morning.

THACKERAY: Why not?

WOOD: I'm a bank manager. Monday is my busy morning.

THACKERAY: This Monday is my busy morning, too.

WOOD: Five people are coming to see me at the bank this morning.

THACKERAY: They'll have to wait, then.

WOOD: They can't wait.

THACKERAY: Your assistant can see them.

WOOD: My assistant can't see them. You don't understand.

THACKERAY: No I'm sorry, Mr Wood, I don't.

WOOD: They have to see the manager. It's a question of money.

THACKERAY: How much?

WOOD: A lot.

THACKERAY: And your assistant can't give it to them?

WOOD: Only the manager can. Please, doctor. I'm all right now. I'm not sick. I must get up.

THACKERAY: I'm not your doctor, Mr Wood.

WOOD: You're not my doctor! Who are you, then?

THACKERAY: Police. Detective Inspector Thackeray.

WOOD: Police! What do *you* want?

THACKERAY: The answers to one or two questions.

WOOD: All right, Inspector.

THACKERAY: Thank you, Mr Wood. Now – what time did you arrive at the store this morning?

WOOD: Quarter to ten. I went straight to the fourth floor.

THACKERAY: Why?

WOOD: The bank is going to open a new office next year. I wanted to buy some tables and chairs.

THACKERAY: And the office furniture is on the fourth floor?

WOOD: That's right. Well – I went straight up there and I started to make my list. (*Pause*)

THACKERAY: Go on.

WOOD: Then I looked up and I saw the fire.

THACKERAY: Where?

WOOD: In the corner of the room.

THACKERAY: So what did you do?

WOOD: I ran straight to the stairs.

THACKERAY: Why didn't you go down them?

WOOD: The smoke stopped me. It was very thick.

THACKERAY: So where did you go?

WOOD: To the lift.

THACKERAY: Ah, yes. I forgot. These stores always have a lift, don't they?

WOOD: Yes, but this one didn't work.

THACKERAY: Oh! Why?

WOOD: I don't know, Inspector. I tried it. The shop assistant tried it. The boy tried it. But it always stopped at the third floor.

THACKERAY: What then?

WOOD: I ran to the telephone.

THACKERAY: Where was that?

WOOD: On the other side of the room. At the front of the

building. In a small office.

THACKERAY: The shop assistant and the boy. What did they do?

WOOD: They followed me.

THACKERAY: I see. So you phoned the fire brigade from the office?

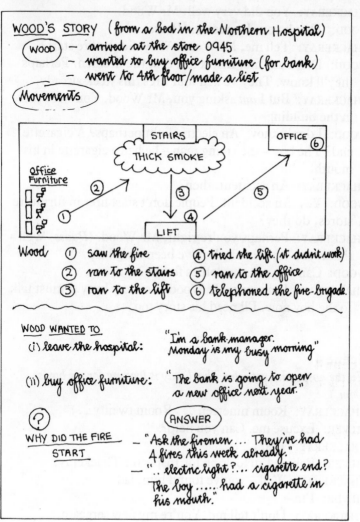

WOOD'S STORY (from a bed in the Northern Hospital)

WOOD — arrived at the store 0945
— wanted to buy office furniture (for bank)
— went to 4th floor/made a list

Movements

Wood
① saw the fire
② ran to the stairs
③ ran to the lift
④ tried the lift. (It didn't work)
⑤ ran to the office
⑥ telephoned the fire-brigade.

WOOD WANTED TO
(i) leave the hospital: "I'm a bank manager. Monday is my busy morning"

(ii) buy office furniture: "The bank is going to open a new office next year."

WHY DID THE FIRE START — ANSWER

— "Ask the firemen ... They've had 4 fires this week already."
— ".. electric light ?... cigarette end? The boy ..... had a cigarette in his mouth."

7

WOOD: Yes.

THACKERAY: Mm. The firemen found you very quickly, didn't they?

WOOD: It was easy for them.

THACKERAY: You gave them the number of the floor.

WOOD: And I told them the right window.

THACKERAY: You did very well, Mr Wood.

WOOD: Thank you, Inspector. (*Pause*)

THACKERAY: Tell me, Mr Wood. Why did the fire start?

WOOD: Don't ask me, Inspector. Ask the firemen. Perhaps they'll know. They've had four fires this week already.

THACKERAY: But I *am* asking you, Mr Wood. You were there in the building.

WOOD: I don't know. An electric light perhaps? A cigarette end? The boy – the young man – he had a cigarette in his mouth.

THACKERAY: An accident, then?

WOOD: Yes. An accident. People don't start fires in furniture stores, do they?

THACKERAY: Perhaps you're right, Mr Wood. (*Pause*) Well – thank you very much. You've been a big help.

WOOD: Can you get my clothes for me?

THACKERAY: I'm sorry, Mr Wood. I'm very busy. I must talk to the boy now. I'll need his story too.

Scene 4

(*In the hospital. Inspector Thackeray is looking for the boy's room.*)

THACKERAY: Room nineteen ... Room twenty ...

SILVER: Excuse me. Can you help?

THACKERAY: Yes?

SILVER: Police. I'm looking for Inspector Thackeray.

THACKERAY: Well – you've found him, lad.

SILVER: I'm –

THACKERAY: Don't tell me. You're my new sergeant.

SILVER: Yes, sir. Alexander Silver. With an 'E–R'.
S-I-L-V-E-R.

THACKERAY: All right, lad. I can spell.

SILVER: Sorry, sir.

THACKERAY: You're late, Sergeant. Why?

SILVER: The fire, sir. It stopped all the traffic. My car didn't move for twenty minutes.

THACKERAY: At your age I had a bicycle.

SILVER: Yes, but –

THACKERAY: How old are you, Sergeant?

SILVER: Twenty-two, sir.

THACKERAY: They made me a sergeant at thirty-four.

SILVER: Those were the old days, sir.

THACKERAY: And they were the good days too, Sergeant. But we mustn't stop here. I'm looking for Room twenty-four. Peter Green.

(*The two men start to walk again.*)

SILVER: He was in the building at the time of the fire?

THACKERAY: He was.

SILVER: And we're going to question him?

THACKERAY: *I'm* going to question him, Sergeant. You can write down the answers.

SILVER: Yes, sir. And then I'll write a report. I'm very good at that, you know. I was first in English at the Police School.

THACKERAY: Were you? (*Pause*) So you write good reports, eh? What was your first name again?

SILVER: My first name? Oh – Alexander, sir.

THACKERAY: Alexander the Great?

SILVER: Did he write good reports too, sir?

THACKERAY: Forget it, Sergeant. Come on. This is Peter Green's room. We'll hear his story now.

Scene 5

(*Peter Green's room. The radio is playing pop music.*)

THACKERAY: Turn that radio off, please.

GREEN: You what?

THACKERAY: I can't ask questions with that noise.

SILVER: I'll turn it off, sir. (*He turns the radio off*)

THACKERAY: Thank you, Silver. Here give it to me.

GREEN: Hey! That's *my* radio.

THACKERAY: You can have it in a minute, son.

GREEN: I'll have it now, dad.

THACKERAY: I'm not your dad. You call me "sir".

GREEN: And I'm not your son. You call me "mister".

THACKERAY: Don't write that down, Silver.

SILVER: Sorry, sir.

THACKERAY: Now, young man. Why were you in the store at the time of the fire?

GREEN: I went to see the old woman.

THACKERAY: The old woman? There wasn't an old woman there. There was only the shop assistant.

GREEN: That's right. That's my old woman.

SILVER: "Old woman", sir – it's just his name for mother.

THACKERAY: Just write the words down, Sergeant.

SILVER: Sorry, sir.

THACKERAY: Tell me, Mister Green. Why did you want to see your mother?

GREEN: I'm forming a group.

THACKERAY: You're what?

GREEN: I'm forming a group. You know – pop music. The Beatles.

THACKERAY: The Beatles?

GREEN: I play the guitar, man. I'm going to be lead guitar.

THACKERAY: *Going* to be . . . ?

GREEN: I haven't got the guitar yet. But I saw this guitar in a music shop this morning. Only £150. Really cheap, man.

THACKERAY: So you went to your mother for the money?

GREEN: That's right. She's got hundreds in the bank.

THACKERAY: And did she give it to you?

GREEN: No.

THACKERAY: So what did you do?

GREEN: I took that radio out of my pocket. And I played some pop music. Very loud.

THACKERAY: She didn't like that?

GREEN: No. People in the shop won't buy the furniture –

THACKERAY: Because they don't like the noise.

GREEN: Yes.

THACKERAY: That man in the fire with you – Mr Wood. Did he buy any furniture?

GREEN: No. He just walked to the other end of the room.

THACKERAY: And your mother?

GREEN: She never said a word.

THACKERAY: So what did you do?

GREEN: I took a cigarette from her handbag. I put it in my mouth. Then I said "Does this place burn easily?"

SILVER: *You* started the fire, then?

GREEN: No. I don't even smoke. I just wanted to frighten her. I needed that £150. But then the *real* fire started.

THACKERAY: Where?

GREEN: Near the stairs. There was a lot of smoke. So we ran to the lift. But it didn't work. And then a second fire started at the end of the room. I tell you, man, that frightened me. Then a third one started. It was nasty. Really nasty.

THACKERAY: So what did you do?

GREEN: We followed Mr Wood to the office.

THACKERAY: And then you phoned.

GREEN: We had to break the door down first.

THACKERAY: Weren't there any windows in the office?

GREEN: Not on the inside.

THACKERAY: Who phoned the fire brigade?

GREEN: Wood. He phoned them. Then he pushed us on the floor. The smoke, you know.

THACKERAY: He was right. You don't get much smoke near the floor.

12

GREEN: That man really helped us.

THACKERAY: And you've helped us too, Mr Green.

SILVER: (*to Thackeray*) Excuse me, sir. Can I ask a question?

GREEN: What do you want to know?

SILVER: Show me your hands, Mr Green. (*Green shows him his left hand.*) Thank you. Now, the right one.

GREEN: Look at those fingers, man. They're just waiting for a guitar.

SILVER: Thank you, Mr Green.

THACKERAY: Come along, Sergeant. (*To Green*) Your radio's on the table there. (*They leave. The Inspector closes the door behind them.*)

SILVER: Mrs Green, next?

THACKERAY: No. We can't see her today. She's not very well.

SILVER: Did you see Green's fingers, sir? The big finger on his right hand was brown. But he said –

THACKERAY: Silver, I want you to go to this address. (*He gives Silver a piece of paper.*)

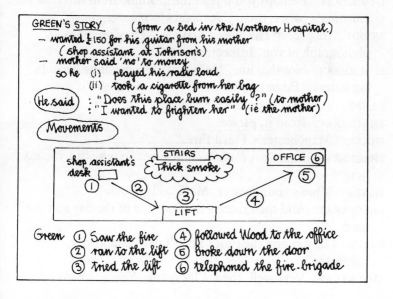

GREEN'S STORY   (from a bed in the Northern Hospital.)
– wanted £150 for his guitar from his mother
    (shop assistant at Johnson's)
– mother said 'no' to money
    so he (i) played his radio loud
            (ii) took a cigarette from her bag
He said : "Does this place burn easily?" (to mother)
         : "I wanted to frighten her" (ie the mother)
Movements

shop assistant's desk | STAIRS Thick smoke | OFFICE ⑥
① ② ③ LIFT ④ ⑤

Green ① Saw the fire   ④ followed Wood to the office
       ② ran to the lift   ⑤ broke down the door
       ③ tried the lift   ⑥ telephoned the fire-brigade

13

SILVER: Is this the name of the arsonist, sir?

THACKERAY: Yes. The address is on the other side.

SILVER: Ah yes, I see.

THACKERAY: I want you to look for any papers or any photographs about fires in Manchester.

SILVER: But, how do you know –?

THACKERAY: How do I know the arsonist? Three things, really. But I'll tell you tomorrow, Sergeant. In my office.

Inspector Thackeray explains

(*The next day. In the Inspector's office.*)

THACKERAY: No, you cannot leave, Mr Wood.

SILVER: Sit down again, please.

THACKERAY: There have been *four* fires in Manchester this week, Mr Wood.

WOOD: I know, Inspector. I told you that.

THACKERAY: But how did you know?

WOOD: From the newspapers.

THACKERAY: Perhaps you'll read the headline from this morning's paper, then. (*He shows him the newspaper.*)

WOOD: "Inspector Thackeray Arrives." They've got a photograph of you, Inspector.

THACKERAY: Not that line, Mr Wood. The headline here. In big letters. (*Pause*)

SILVER: You're very quiet, Mr Wood.

THACKERAY: Read it, please.

WOOD: "Manchester's Third Fire."

THACKERAY: Exactly. (*Pause*) *Third* Fire. So why did you say four?

SILVER: What's your answer, Mr Wood? (*Pause*)

THACKERAY: And then there's the question of the day and the time.

WOOD: The day and the time? I don't understand you, Inspector.

THACKERAY: Very well, then. I'll explain. You're a bank

manager, Mr Wood. Monday is a busy morning for you. You had to see five people at the bank this Monday. But you went to a furniture store. Why?

WOOD: I've told you. I had to buy some furniture for the bank.

THACKERAY: But you only need the furniture *next year*. Why did you have to go this Monday morning?

SILVER: Why didn't you send your assistant, Mr Wood? (*Pause*)

THACKERAY: You don't want to answer? All right, then. We'll talk about the telephone now.

WOOD: The telephone?

THACKERAY: You were on the fourth floor of a furniture store. There was a bad fire. The lift didn't work. So you phoned for help.

WOOD: That's right.

THACKERAY: Tell me, Mr Wood. Where was that telephone?

WOOD: In the office at the front of the building. I told you that yesterday, Inspector.

THACKERAY: Yes, you did. But how did you know?

WOOD: Well -er – em – I saw it there.

THACKERAY: You looked through the office window?

WOOD: Yes. That's right.

THACKERAY: The office doesn't have any windows, Mr Wood. Not on the inside.

WOOD: Perhaps I saw it through the door.

THACKERAY: You had to break the door down, Mr Wood. (*Pause*) Sergeant.

SILVER: Yes, sir.

THACKERAY: Show Mr Wood those drawings.

SILVER: Yes, sir. I found these drawings in your house yesterday, Mr Wood.

THACKERAY: They show the fourth floor of Johnson's Furniture Store.

SILVER: The stairs, the lift, the offices – you know that floor very well.

THACKERAY: Tell me, Mr Wood. How many fires were there on that floor?

WOOD: Er – three, I think. Yes, three. But –

THACKERAY: There are three crosses on your drawing.

(*A knock at the door*)

CONSTABLE: Excuse me, sir.

THACKERAY: Ah, come in, Constable. Take Mr Wood into the next room. Then write down his name, his age, his date of birth – the usual things – on this paper. Then – in ten minutes – I'll come in and, Mr Wood, you'll give me the true story.

CONSTABLE: Come along, Mr Wood.

WOOD: Yes, Constable. (*He stops at the door*) Inspector.

THACKERAY: Yes, Mr Wood?

WOOD: My wife and children . . . . . .

THACKERAY: Yes, Mr Wood?

WOOD: I love them. I love them very much.

CONSTABLE: Come along, sir. You can talk about your family later. (*They go out.*)

SILVER: Why did he say that, sir?

THACKERAY: About his wife and children?

SILVER: Yes.

THACKERAY: They've left him. They left him last month. It's the old, old story, Sergeant. The man works long hours. The wife never sees him. So she leaves.

SILVER: So he started the fires because –

THACKERAY: Because he loves his family and his family have left him.

SILVER: But I don't understand. Why start a fire?

THACKERAY: I don't know. I'm a policeman, not a psychologist. Ask the psychologists. Ask the doctors. Perhaps they can explain it.

SILVER: Are you going to see Peter Green again, sir? His story was wrong too, you know.

THACKERAY: The big finger on his right hand.

SILVER: Yes, sir. It was brown. And he said "I don't even smoke". I have his exact words here. I wrote them down.

THACKERAY: He doesn't smoke *now*, Silver. He stopped last month. You'll find it in his medical file at the hospital.

SILVER: His medical file! They didn't tell us about medical files in the Police School.

THACKERAY: Did they tell you about tea, Sergeant?

SILVER: Tea? No, sir.

THACKERAY: The tea-pot's behind those files there. The cups are on the table behind you. And I like it strong.

17

Airport Kidnap

Characters

Inspector Thackeray
Sergeant Silver
Mr Martin, head teacher
Airport Information Desk assistant
Miss Grant, Sheikh Rahman's air hostess
Fatima, Sheikh Rahman's daughter
Airport radio announcer
Mrs Evans, assistant at the airport shop
Air hostess
First pilot
Second pilot
Air traffic controller

Scene 1

(*Manchester Airport, Information Desk.*)

THACKERAY: His name is York. Chief Inspector York.

SILVER: And it's Gate Number 2, isn't it?

THACKERAY: That's right, Silver.

SILVER: When does his plane arrive, sir?

THACKERAY: The Information Desk here will tell you that.

ASSISTANT: Good morning, sir.

SILVER: Good morning, miss. I want to know the time of –

MARTIN: Quick. I need your help. It's very important.

ASSISTANT: (*to Mr Martin*) Wait a minute please, sir.

MARTIN: This boy. Abdulla Mohammed Abdul Rahman.
Look – this is his photograph. (*He shows the photograph to the assistant*) I can't find him.

THACKERAY: Abdul Rahman. I know that name, don't I?

MARTIN: His father's an oil sheikh.

THACKERAY: Sheikh Mohammed Abdul Rahman, isn't it?
What's his son doing in Britain?

18

MARTIN: He goes to my school.

THACKERAY: And you are –?

MARTIN: John Martin. Head teacher. (*To the assistant*) Please, miss. Will you –

ASSISTANT: I'll just finish with this other gentleman first.

MARTIN: But you don't understand, miss. He's disappeared.

ASSISTANT: Disappeared?

MARTIN: He's gone, I tell you. Gone.

THACKERAY: You've searched the building, Mr Martin?

MARTIN: Of course I've searched the building. I've looked in the waiting-rooms, in the airport shops, in the –

SILVER: Where did you leave him?

MARTIN: At our table in the restaurant.

SILVER: Who with?

MARTIN: His sister and the air hostess.

THACKERAY: Why did you do that?

MARTIN: I had to go to the airport bank. I was only there for two or three minutes. Then I came back. And – and –

THACKERAY: That passport in your hand – it's the boy's, isn't it?

MARTIN: Yes.

THACKERAY: Can I look at it, please? We're police. Detective Inspector Thackeray. And this is Sergeant Silver.

MARTIN: Here you are, Inspector. And you can have this photograph of him as well.

THACKERAY: Thank you, Mr Martin.

SILVER: The passport is Saudi Arabian, I see.

THACKERAY: I want the page with the description on it. Here we are. "Description". Nine years of age. One metre fifty.

SILVER: That's four feet eleven inches.

THACKERAY: Brown eyes and black hair.

MARTIN: There's a story in the newspapers about kidnappers every day, Inspector. You *will* find him for me, won't you?

ASSISTANT: Kidnappers! Why didn't you say that earlier? Perhaps I can help.

MARTIN: Please, miss.

ASSISTANT: We have the airport radio here. I can read out the name and the description of the boy for you.

SILVER: Yes. Then all the airport police will be able to look for him, too.

THACKERAY: No. Don't do that, miss. Telephone them.

MARTIN: Then the kidnappers won't hear.

ASSISTANT: All right, sir. I'll do it now.

THACKERAY: And I'll go to the restaurant. That air hostess will still be there, won't she?

MARTIN: Yes, Inspector.

THACKERAY: Perhaps she'll be able to help. You come along too, Mr Martin.

Scene 2

(*The airport restaurant.*)

THACKERAY: So, Miss Grant. The Sheikh has his own plane.

MISS GRANT: That's right, Inspector. And I'm his air hostess.

FATIMA: When can we go home?

MARTIN: We must find your brother first, Fatima.

FATIMA: I want to go home.

THACKERAY: Answer my questions, Fatima; then maybe you will.

FATIMA: All right, Inspector.

THACKERAY: Now – your brother Abdulla: where did you see him last?

FATIMA: In front of that shop.

SILVER: Brown's? The clothes shop?

MISS GRANT: Yes, that's right. We walked to it from this table.

FATIMA: I bought a bag there. Look. It's nice, isn't it?

MISS GRANT: We were only in there for three or four minutes.

MARTIN: I was in the bank then. Oh, but of course, I've told you that already, haven't I?

THACKERAY: You're writing all this down in your notebook, Sergeant?

SILVER: Yes, sir.

MISS GRANT: Then we walked out of the shop and back to the table here. But –

THACKERAY: But Abdulla wasn't with you.

MISS GRANT: No, Inspector. He wasn't. So I started to look for him.

MARTIN: And then I arrived from the bank.

THACKERAY: Mm. I see. (*Pause*) Fatima.

FATIMA: Yes, Inspector?

THACKERAY: You wanted a bag. So you went to that shop and you bought one. Tell me – what did Abdulla want to buy?

FATIMA: Chocolate. He wanted to buy some chocolate.

MARTIN: You never told *me* that.

FATIMA: You never asked me that.

SILVER: But which shop sells chocolate?

MISS GRANT: Smith's. The one behind us there.

THACKERAY: You did look in there, didn't you, Mr Martin?

MARTIN: I looked in all the shops.

THACKERAY: And did you talk to the assistants?

MARTIN: I didn't have time.

AIRPORT RADIO: Flight AVC 234 to Al Azrak. Last call for Flight AVC 234. Will passengers please go to Gate Number 24. Flight AVC 234 to Al Azrak.

THACKERAY: Flight to Al Azrak, eh?

SILVER: That isn't Saudi Arabia, is it?

THACKERAY: No. It's north Ketaba. I don't like it, Silver.

SILVER: What can we do, sir?

THACKERAY: Stop it.

SILVER: How?

THACKERAY: Go to Gate 24.

SILVER: Me, sir? But –

THACKERAY: Yes. You, Silver. And search that plane.

SILVER: But where are *you* going?

THACKERAY: To the shop. Hurry, Silver. You haven't got much time.

Air-hostess in Sheikh Abdul Rahman's plane.

MISS GRANT
- *walked with Fatima & Abdulla to the shop*
- *said : "We were only in there 3 or 4 minutes."*
- *returned with Fatima to the restaurant table.*

BUT — ABDULLA WASN'T THERE !!!

Abdulla's younger sister. She goes to the same school

FATIMA
- *walked to Brown's shop (with Abd. & Miss Gr.)*
- *bought a bag; returned to the table.*
- *said : "Abdulla wanted to buy some chocolate"*

SMITH'S SHOP SELLS CHOCOLATE !!!

Scene 3

(*Smith's, the airport shop.*)

THACKERAY: Have a good look at the photograph, Mrs Evans. Brown eyes, black hair, a long thin face.

MRS EVANS: I never remember faces, Inspector. I often get three or four hundred people here in a day. This shop's very busy, you know.

THACKERAY: A schoolboy. Four feet, eleven inches –

MRS EVANS: We get a lot of schoolboys in here.

THACKERAY: He was in a grey school uniform.

MRS EVANS: Was he? My little Peter wears a grey school uniform. He's nine too.

THACKERAY: I'm not looking for your little Peter, Mrs Evans.

MRS EVANS: No. You're not, are you?

THACKERAY: I'm looking for the boy in this photograph.

MRS EVANS: And his kidnappers.

THACKERAY: And I haven't got much time.

MRS EVANS: Mm – oh yes, I remember now. I did have *one* boy in the shop this morning. He bought one of those games.

THACKERAY: Was he in a school uniform?

MRS EVANS: Yes, but he wasn't your Saudi Arabian.

THACKERAY: How do you know that?

MRS EVANS: He had red hair.
   (*Pause*)
THACKERAY: Have you sold any chocolate this morning?
MRS EVANS: Oh yes.
THACKERAY: In the last quarter of an hour?
MRS EVANS: Ye-es. I sold one of those large boxes of chocolates
   there. And I –
THACKERAY: Who to?
MRS EVANS: Who to? It was – er – It was – er . . .
THACKERAY: Try to remember, Mrs Evans. It's very
   important.
MRS EVANS: I'm sorry, Inspector. I can't. But – er –
THACKERAY: But what, Mrs Evans? *Please*, go on.
MRS EVANS: There were six bars of chocolate, this morning.
   Now who did I sell that to?
THACKERAY: Have another look at the photograph.
MRS EVANS: Yes. I remember him now. It *was* your Saudi
   Arabian. He bought six bars of milk chocolate.

24

MRS EVANS

She is the shop assistant at Smith's. She talks a lot and she remembers things v. slowly.

— said: (about her son), "My little Peter wears a grey school uniform. He's 9 too."

— said: Abdulla "bought 6 bars of milk chocolate".

— said: "He also bought a book on aeroplanes. ..... He wanted to read it on the plane."

THACKERAY: Where did he go?

MRS EVANS: And a book. He bought a book, as well.

THACKERAY: *But where did he go?*

MRS EVANS: A book about planes. He wanted to read it on the plane.

THACKERAY: He spoke to you?

MRS EVANS: Yes. And he said —

THACKERAY: Don't stop. What did he say?

MRS EVANS: He liked planes. That was it. He liked to watch planes.

THACKERAY: How did he leave the shop? By that door there?

MRS EVANS: Oh, no. That door doesn't open. The conveyor belt is behind it.

THACKERAY: The conveyor belt?

MRS EVANS: It carries the passenger's bags and cases. They go to the ground floor. Then the lorries take them to the planes.

THACKERAY: So he went out by the door at the front.

MRS EVANS: Yes. And I'll tell you another thing. You see those stairs. He walked up those stairs. I remember it very well now.

THACKERAY: Those stairs. They go to the airport roof, don't they?

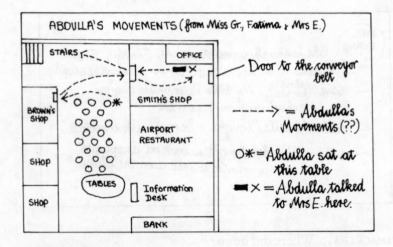

ABDULLA'S MOVEMENTS (from Miss Gr., Fatima & Mrs E.)

STAIRS

OFFICE

Door to the conveyor belt

BROWN'S SHOP

SMITH'S SHOP

AIRPORT RESTAURANT

-----> = Abdulla's Movements (??)

O✳ = Abdulla sat at this table

■✕ = Abdulla talked to Mrs E. here.

SHOP

SHOP

TABLES

Information Desk

BANK

MRS EVANS: Yes. A lot of people watch the planes from up
   there. (*The Inspector leaves the shop quickly.*) Hey –
   Inspector – wait a minute, please. I want to ask you a
   question.

THACKERAY: Later, Mrs Evans. I must find the head teacher
   again.

MRS EVANS: But where are you going?

THACKERAY: To the Control Tower, Mrs Evans. I'm going to
   the airport Control Tower with the head teacher.

Scene 4

(*Flight AVC 234. In the aircraft.*)

AIR HOSTESS: Well – you've seen all the passengers, Sergeant.
   The boy's not here.

SILVER: I must talk to the pilot now.

AIR HOSTESS: There won't be time for that. We have to take
   off in one minute.

SILVER: The cabin's this way, isn't it? (*He walks to the cabin.*)

AIR HOSTESS: The cabin? You can't go in there, Sergeant. (*She
   walks after him.*) Only the pilots can go in the cabin.

SILVER: I'm sorry, miss. I must. (*He goes into the cabin.*)

26

FIRST PILOT: (*switches on an engine*) First engine: working at full power.

SECOND PILOT: (*switches on an engine*) Second engine: working at full power.

FIRST PILOT: Control Tower. This is Flight Able Victor Charlie 234. Flight Able Victor Charlie 234. All our engines are working. We're ready for take-off. Repeat. Ready for take-off.

SILVER: I'm sorry, gentlemen. You can't take off yet. Please switch off the engines.

FIRST PILOT: Who are you?

SILVER: Police. Sergeant Silver. Manchester C.I.D.

SECOND PILOT: And what are you doing here?

AIR HOSTESS: He's looking for a young boy.

FIRST PILOT: Well, *we* haven't got him.

SECOND PILOT: There's no boy on this aircraft, is there?

AIR HOSTESS: We've searched the plane, sir.

FIRST PILOT: And you didn't find him.

AIR HOSTESS: No, we didn't.

FIRST PILOT: Then you must leave now, Sergeant.

SILVER: I can't do that, sir.

SECOND PILOT: Oh, can't you?

FIRST PILOT: Then you'll have to come to Al Azrak with us.

CONTROL TOWER: Flight Able Victor Charlie 234. Go to runway one. Repeat. Go to runway one. Over.

FIRST PILOT: You heard the message from the Control Tower.

SECOND PILOT: Are you leaving, Sergeant?

FIRST PILOT: Or are you coming with us?

SILVER: I've told you. This plane must not take off. (*He walks to the first pilot.*)

AIR HOSTESS: Sergeant – what are you –?

FIRST PILOT: Don't touch those switches, man.

SECOND PILOT: Stop him.

AIR HOSTESS: He's switching off the engines!

FIRST PILOT: (*stands up*) Get out of this cabin. Do you hear me? Get out.

27

AIR HOSTESS: Will you please leave, Sergeant.

CONTROL TOWER: Flight Able Victor Charlie 234. There is a delay in your flight. Repeat. There is a delay in your flight. Please switch off your engines and wait. We have the police here. Over.

SILVER: Now perhaps you'll listen to me. I tell you – we're trying to find a young . . . .

Scene 5

(*In the Control Tower.*)

MARTIN: You can't see the plane very well from this side of the Control Tower, Inspector.

THACKERAY: It has stopped, hasn't it?

AIR TRAFFIC CONTROLLER (A.T.C.): You heard my message, didn't you?

THACKERAY: *I* heard it. Did the pilot?

FIRST PILOT: (*on the radio*) Control Tower. Able Victor Charlie here. We've stopped the plane. Over.

A.T.C.: Thank you, Able Victor Charlie. Over.

FIRST PILOT: We have a Police Sergeant here. Some story about a kidnap. Over.

THACKERAY: Can I speak to him?

A.T.C.: Yes. Here you are.

THACKERAY: Control Tower. Inspector Thackeray here. Has my Sergeant found the boy? Over.

FIRST PILOT: No. But we've searched the plane. Over.

THACKERAY: Search it again, please. And look in the baggage hold. Repeat. Look in the baggage hold. Over and out.

MARTIN: The baggage hold!

THACKERAY: That's right, Mr Martin.

A.T.C.: The place for the bags and cases.

MARTIN: But he won't be there, will he?

THACKERAY: We'll know in a minute, won't we?

A.T.C.: This boy, Mr Martin. He's Saudi Arabian, isn't he?

MARTIN: Yes. I told you that before, didn't I?

A.T.C.: His English is good, is it?

MARTIN: Not bad.

A.T.C.: Can he ask for help?

MARTIN: Oh, yes. He speaks quite well.

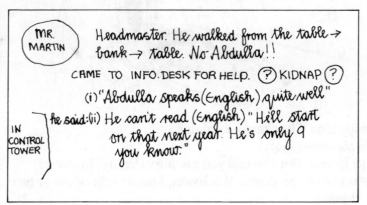

THACKERAY: Does he read and write?

MARTIN: Not in English. Not yet. He'll start on that next year. He's only nine, you know.

SILVER: (*on the radio*) We've found him, sir. Oh – sorry! Control Tower. Able Victor Charlie here. We've found him. In a large case in the baggage hold. He's sleeping. He won't wake up. Can you hear me, sir? – – Are you there? Oh – sorry! Over.

THACKERAY: Control Tower here. Thackeray. Well done, Silver. Wait in the aeroplane. I'm going to question the kidnappers. Over and out.

MARTIN: You're going to question the –! But you don't know them yet.

THACKERAY: I do, Mr Martin. I know them very well. Very well indeed.

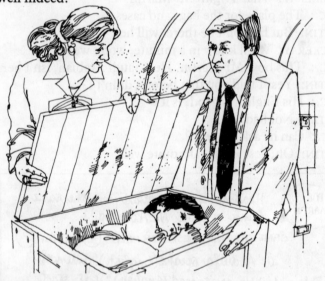

Inspector Thackeray explains

(*In the airport shop*.)

MRS EVANS: But I've told you my story already, Inspector.

THACKERAY: Sit down, Mrs Evans. I have to check one or two things.

MRS EVANS: Go on, then. But be quick. I must open this shop again in a minute.

THACKERAY: You said: "The boy bought a book!"

MRS EVANS: Did I?

THACKERAY: You can check the words in my notebook here.

MRS EVANS: Ah, yes. I remember now. He bought a book about planes. He wanted to read it on the plane.

THACKERAY: No, Mrs Evans. That can't be right.

MRS EVANS: Why not?

THACKERAY: The boy can't read.

MRS EVANS: How do you know that?

THACKERAY: I checked it with the head teacher. (*Pause*) But that's not all. See this word here? At the bottom of the page.

MRS EVANS: Yes. It says – "kidnappers". You've put a circle round it.

THACKERAY: Tell me, Mrs Evans. Why did you talk about kidnappers?

MRS EVANS: Why did *you* ask all those questions?

THACKERAY: I never used the word "kidnappers". So where did you get it from?

MRS EVANS: Perhaps I – er –

THACKERAY: And how did you know the boy's age?

MRS EVANS: I didn't, Inspector.

THACKERAY: "He's nine," you said. I have your words here. And then there's his nationality.

MRS EVANS: His nationality? But we all know that. He's Saudi Arabian.

THACKERAY: I never told you, Mrs Evans.

MRS EVANS: What *are* you trying to tell me, Inspector?

THACKERAY: You kidnapped the boy, didn't you?

MRS EVANS: Inspector! I was here in the shop all the time.

THACKERAY: You used that conveyor belt.

MRS EVANS: The door to it won't open. You know that.

THACKERAY: The engineers can open it.

MRS EVANS: Can they?

THACKERAY: Yes. And I have a list of their names here.

MRS EVANS: Do you?

THACKERAY: One of the names is Evans. Airport Engineer Evans. (*Pause*) He's your husband, isn't he? (*Pause*) Isn't he?

MRS EVANS: Yes. But I still don't understand. How did I kidnap that boy?

THACKERAY: It was easy. He came into your shop. You gave him some chocolate. He ate it, and then he asked to sit down.

MRS EVANS: He asked to sit down! Why?

THACKERAY: He was tired. He wanted to go to sleep.

MRS EVANS: At eleven o'clock in the morning! Why?

THACKERAY: Your chocolate did it. (*Pause*) So you took him into your office. Mr Evans was already in there. He had a large case on the floor.

MRS EVANS: You can really tell a good story, Inspector!

THACKERAY: A minute later, the boy was asleep.

MRS EVANS: Inspector!

THACKERAY: You put the boy in the case, and you put the top back on it again. Then Mr Evans opened the door to the conveyor belt and –

MRS EVANS: But I'm not the kidnapper. I tried to help you.

THACKERAY: You didn't, Mrs Evans.

MRS EVANS: I did. I answered all your questions.

THACKERAY: You wanted to keep me in your shop.

MRS EVANS: No, Inspector. No.

THACKERAY: I came here at eleven o'clock. The plane to Al Azrak always takes off at quarter past eleven. You wanted to keep me here for those fifteen minutes.

MRS EVANS: Where's my husband, Inspector?

THACKERAY: At the police station.

MRS EVANS: I want to see him.

THACKERAY: Later, Mrs Evans. Later. First I want some names and addresses. This kidnap was a big job. It needed four or five people. I want the names of those people, Mrs Evans. And I want them now.

The Electronic Eye

Characters

Inspector Thackeray
Sergeant Silver
Miss Day, journalist for the "Manchester News"
Professor Lane, electronics expert
Taxi driver
Mr Haffner, businessman
Miss Jones, secretary to the Professor
Miss Lane, the Professor's daughter

Scene 1

(*The office of the "Manchester News".*)

THACKERAY: So, Miss Day. There'll be no story about this in tonight's "Manchester News", will there?

MISS DAY: *I'm* not going to write one, Inspector.

THACKERAY: And your man outside Professor Lane's House? Is *he*?

MISS DAY: Who told you about him?

THACKERAY: I'm asking the questions, miss. (*The Inspector's radio buzzes. He answers.*) Thackeray here. Over.

SILVER: Sergeant Silver. I'm still outside Professor Lane's house. A man's just arrived in a taxi. He's going into the house. Over.

THACKERAY: And the other man? From the "Manchester News"? Is he still there? Over.

SILVER: Yes. In the doorway of the church. He's writing in his notebook. He hasn't moved all day. Over.

THACKERAY: I'll come straight to you from the "Manchester News" office. In about quarter of an hour. Over and out.

MISS DAY: So, Inspector. *You* have a man in front of the house, too?

34

THACKERAY: That's right, miss.

MISS DAY: This Professor Lane, then. What do you know about him?

THACKERAY: His work is top-secret, Miss Day.

MISS DAY: Military electronics always is top-secret.

THACKERAY: Then why are you asking me?

MISS DAY: He works for the government, doesn't he?

THACKERAY: He *worked* for the government.

MISS DAY: And now?

THACKERAY: He works for "Lane Military Electronics."

MISS DAY: His own company, is it?

THACKERAY: Yes. His own company. But that's no secret. You'll find it in the telephone book on your desk there. A one-man, one-month-old company. It sells electronic ideas.

MISS DAY: Who to?

THACKERAY: Only the Professor knows that.

MISS DAY: But now our government wants to know. Is that it?

THACKERAY: His ideas mustn't go to the wrong people, must they? (*The Inspector's radio buzzes.*) Thackeray here. Over.

SILVER: MI5 has just telephoned. They've got the name of the visitor. It's a Mr Paul Haffner. He sells electronics to military governments. Very friendly with the President of Mubalia. He flew in from Switzerland yesterday lunchtime. Over.

THACKERAY: Stay in the car, Silver. I'm coming now. Over and out. I'll have to leave, Miss Day. Remember, now – no newspaper stories.

MISS DAY: I know – it's all top-secret.

THACKERAY: And it must stay top-secret, too.

Scene 2

(*Outside Professor Lane's house. The two policemen are in the police car.*)

SILVER: That's the house, sir. Thirty-nine Ash Road. The one with the big garden.

THACKERAY: Ah, yes. I can see the number on the front gate.

SILVER: Wait a minute, sir. The door's opening.

THACKERAY: Now who can that be?

SILVER: Haffner. Yes, it's Paul Haffner. He's coming out of the house.

THACKERAY: In a hurry, too.

SILVER: Hello! That's his taxi.

THACKERAY: Where?

SILVER: There, sir. Next to that tree on the other side of the road. It's just driven up.

THACKERAY: Stop it. Quick, Silver.

SILVER: Yes, sir. (*The sergeant drives the car quickly across the road. He stops it just in front of the taxi.*)

TAXI DRIVER: Hey! What are you playing at? This is Ash Road, you know, not Monaco.

(*The sergeant goes to the taxi driver; the Inspector goes to the gate of the house.*)

SILVER: Police. You'll have to –

TAXI DRIVER: French Police?

SILVER: Don't be funny.

TAXI DRIVER: We drive on the left in Britain, you know.

SILVER: Stay there. And don't move. (*He goes to the Inspector at the gate.*)

HAFFNER: Move to one side, please. My taxi's waiting.

THACKERAY: You're Mr Paul Haffner, sir?

HAFFNER: I'm in a hurry, I tell you. I have to go to the airport.

THACKERAY: Police, sir. We'll try to be quick. Just one or two questions.

SILVER: We're only doing our job, sir. We won't take long.

HAFFNER: All right, then. I'll give you five minutes.

THACKERAY: Thank you, sir. We'll go into the house now. We can talk easily there. And I have to see Professor Lane, too.

Scene 3

(*Professor Lane's sitting room.*)

SECRETARY: (*opens the door*) Professor Lane, the police are here, sir.

PROFESSOR: Thank you, Miss Jones. (*To the policemen*) Come in, please.

(*The three men come into the room. The secretary leaves.*)

THACKERAY: I'm Inspector Thackeray. This is Sergeant Silver. Mr Haffner, you already know.

PROFESSOR: Ah, good. You've got him, then.

SILVER: Got who, sir?

PROFESSOR: Haffner.

THACKERAY: Why do you say that?

PROFESSOR: He's stolen my drawings. I've just telephoned the police about it. Didn't you get the message?

HAFFNER: Stolen your drawings?! Really, Professor! Now why do you say that?

PROFESSOR: Why? I'll tell you "why". We were in this room. Remember? And you asked me that question.

SILVER: What about, sir? (*Pause*)

THACKERAY: The question, Professor Lane. What was it about? (*Pause*)

HAFFNER: The electronic eye.

THACKERAY: The electronic eye? What's that, Professor? (*Pause*)

PROFESSOR: I can't answer you, Inspector. It's secret.

THACKERAY: All right, then. We'll go back to your story. Mr Haffner here asked you a question about the electronic eye. What then?

PROFESSOR: I had to check on one or two things. So I went to the office safe.

THACKERAY: And the drawings weren't there.

PROFESSOR: No. They weren't. So I closed the safe and then I came back here.

SILVER: And what did you find?

PROFESSOR: An empty room.

THACKERAY: Well, Mr Haffner. (*Pause*) We're waiting for your answer.

HAFFNER: My answer to what?

THACKERAY: Why did you leave so quickly?

SILVER: You didn't say "goodbye".

HAFFNER: My plane. It was a question of time. The Professor left the room. Then I waited and waited and –

THACKERAY: How long?

HAFFNER: Five minutes, maybe.

THACKERAY: That's not long.

HAFFNER: You don't understand, Inspector. It was already two o'clock. My plane leaves at three. It's a twenty-minute journey to the airport. And our talk was at an end, really.

THACKERAY: Oh! Why was that?

HAFFNER: I can't raise the money.

SILVER: What money?

HAFFNER: The money for the electronic eye. The Professor wants three hundred thousand pounds.

PROFESSOR: But it will make millions and millions of pounds for us.

HAFFNER: I can only raise one hundred thousand.

SECRETARY: (*opens the door*) The "Manchester News" is on the telephone for you, Professor.

THACKERAY: My sergeant will talk to them, Miss Jones. The Professor mustn't answer any questions. Just tell them that, Silver. Give them my name. They'll understand. Then come back here and write down Mr Haffner's story.

SILVER: Yes, sir (*He leaves with Miss Jones.*)

THACKERAY: Now, Professor, I'll have to talk to all the people in the house. There's your secretary and – er – is your wife at home?

PROFESSOR: My wife died last year, Inspector. But there's my daughter. She's here.

THACKERAY: Yes. I'll have to see her as well. In your office, please. It won't take long.

Scene 4

(*The Professor's office.*)

THACKERAY: So you're going to leave this job, Miss Jones.

SECRETARY: At the end of the month, Inspector.

THACKERAY: What will you do then?

SECRETARY: I'll look for a real secretary's job.

THACKERAY: You've got a real secretary's job here, haven't you? (*Secretary laughs.*) Why do you laugh, Miss Jones?

SECRETARY: Real secretaries open letters, answer telephone calls, make appointments.

THACKERAY: And you don't do any of these things.

SECRETARY: No. I don't.

THACKERAY: What do you do then?

SECRETARY: I type. Just type.

THACKERAY: What do you type?

SECRETARY: Figures. Line after line of figures.

THACKERAY: You answer *some* letters, don't you?

SECRETARY: Answer them? (*She laughs.*) I never even open them. They're all top-secret, you know.

THACKERAY: Those figures. They're top-secret. You see those.

SECRETARY: That doesn't matter.

THACKERAY: Why not?

SECRETARY: I can't understand them.

THACKERAY: So you can't remember them. Is that it?

SECRETARY: Yes. That's it.

THACKERAY: Tell me, Miss Jones. Does the Professor have a safe in this room?

SECRETARY: Yes. He puts all his drawings and his papers in it.

THACKERAY: I don't see it here. Where is it?

SECRETARY: I don't know, Inspector.

THACKERAY: You don't know! But you're his secretary. You work here.

SECRETARY: The safe's top-secret, as well. He never opens it in front of me. I always have to leave the room.

THACKERAY: You have to leave the room! (*Pause*) Tell me. Mr Haffner. Does *he* know about the safe?

SECRETARY: Mr Haffner? Who's he?

THACKERAY: The man in the sitting room.

SECRETARY: Oh, that's his name, is it?

THACKERAY: What about the daughter? Does she know about the safe?

SECRETARY: She never comes in here. And anyway the Professor *never* talks about his work to others.

THACKERAY: Doesn't he? (*Pause*)

SECRETARY: Can I go now, Inspector?

THACKERAY: There's just one other thing.

SECRETARY: What's that?

THACKERAY: Your last job. Where was it?

SECRETARY: At the "Manchester News". The work was all right but I had to stay very late in the evenings. My family didn't like that.

THACKERAY: Thank you, Miss Jones. You've been very helpful. (*Pause*) The Professor's daughter can come in now.

Scene 5

(*A few minutes later*)

THACKERAY: So, you teach mathematics at the University of Manchester?

MISS LANE: That's right, Inspector.

THACKERAY: Do you ever help your father in his work?

MISS LANE: (*angrily*) No. Never. Really, Inspector. What a question! (*Pause*)

THACKERAY: Tell me, Miss Lane. Why are you so angry?

MISS LANE: (*quietly*) That electronic eye. It can kill people, you know. Hundreds, thousands of people.

THACKERAY: So *you* took your father's papers then.

MISS LANE: No, Inspector. I'm not a thief.

THACKERAY: Who is the thief, then?

MISS LANE: You're the policeman. You tell me. (*Pause*). But there is one thing.

THACKERAY: What's that?

MISS LANE: Last night. About one o'clock. I heard a noise.

THACKERAY: Where?

MISS LANE: Downstairs. I was in bed at the time.

THACKERAY: So, what did you do?

MISS LANE: I got up and I looked out of the window. It was dark at first. But then a light came on.

THACKERAY: Oh! Where?

MISS LANE: From this office.

THACKERAY: How long was the light on?

MISS LANE: About three minutes, maybe.

THACKERAY: A thief can't do much in three minutes.

MISS LANE: He can find the safe.

THACKERAY: Yes, but then he has to open it.

MISS LANE: That's quite easy. It's an old one, you know.

THACKERAY: Maybe it was your father.

MISS LANE: I asked him this morning. He slept all through the night.

THACKERAY: You didn't tell him about the light and the noise?

MISS LANE: No. I didn't want to –

SILVER: (*comes into the room quickly*) I've got Haffner's story here, sir. And I asked him two or three other questions. You'll find the answers on this piece of paper.

THACKERAY: Thank you, Silver. (*He takes the piece of paper and reads through it.*) Mm – he's worked as an electronics engineer – and what do we have here? He once sold safes? For a company in Switzerland. Well – well – well.

SILVER: So we can –

THACKERAY: Yes. We can take the thief to the police station now. But you must call at the "Manchester News" office, Sergeant. Ask them for the Professor's papers. They can go back in his safe again now.

Haffner:
: First sold safes (!!) Then electronics
: Came to Manchester from Switzerland yesterday.
: Talked with Prof. Lane about electronic eye.
: Left early because
  (i) "My plane leaves at three"
  (ii) "I can't raise the money" (£300,000 for the electronic eye)
: Says he is not the Thief

Prof. Lane. Electronics expert. Talked to Haffner about electronic eye. Left the room. Went to his safe. Opened it. NO DRAWINGS!! Returned to room. NO HAFFNER!! Says: Haffner "has stolen my drawings".

? MISS JONES   **?** MISS LANE

MISS JONES

Secretary. Will leave at the end of the month because
(i) She **cannot** answer telephone calls, open letters, put things in the safe (TOP SECRET)
(ii) She can **only** type

Says
"Prof. never talks about his work to others"
"The safe is top secret"

LAST JOB: Manchester News.!!

MISS LANE

University Lecturer (Maths)
Says "Electronic Eye can kill"
Does not like it.

Last night

She heard a noise downstairs

"A light came on... from this office." (for 3 minutes)

Thief can easily open the safe. Because "It's an old one, you know."

44

Inspector Thackeray explains

(*The Professor's office, ten minutes later.*)

MISS LANE: I'm *not* a thief, Inspector. How many times do I have to tell you?

THACKERAY: You took those drawings.

MISS LANE: Look, Inspector. I've told you my story –

THACKERAY: And it's not a very good one.

MISS LANE: Now why do you say that, Inspector?

THACKERAY: I have my notebook here, Miss Lane. I wrote down one or two things.

MISS LANE: Good. I won't have to repeat them, will I?

THACKERAY: You said – and I have your words here – "this electronic eye can kill people".

MISS LANE: Well? It can.

THACKERAY: How did you know that? (*Pause*) You didn't help your father, did you?

MISS LANE: Er – no.

THACKERAY: And he never spoke about his work, did he? (*Pause*) It was all top-secret, wasn't it? (*Pause*) Wasn't it? (*Pause*) But you knew the name for this – er this electronic thing. And you knew –

MISS LANE: I'm not a thief, Inspector, I tell you.

THACKERAY: And then there's the question of the safe.

MISS LANE: What about it, Inspector?

THACKERAY: You never went into your father's office, did you?

MISS LANE: No, I didn't.

THACKERAY: Then how did you know about the safe? You even said – (*He looks in his notebook*) Where is it, now? Ah yes, here it is – You even said "It's an old one." Tell me. How did you know that?

SILVER: (*opens the door*) You were right, sir.

THACKERAY: Ah, come in, Silver. Come in. (*The Sergeant comes in.*)

SILVER: I've got them.

MISS LANE: Got what?

SILVER: The drawings. They arrived by second post at the "Manchester News" offices this morning.

THACKERAY: Thank you, Sergeant. (*He takes the envelope and turns to Miss Lane.*) Now Miss Lane – tell me. Why did you send these drawings to the "Manchester News"?

MISS LANE: You tell me, Inspector. You know all the answers.

THACKERAY: You wanted to stop the sale of the electronic eye, didn't you? (*Pause*) That was it, wasn't it? (*Pause*) And at the same time you wanted to stop your father's work.

MISS LANE: A letter to the "Manchester News" won't do that.

THACKERAY: A story in the newspaper will.

SILVER: His work won't be top-secret then, will it?

THACKERAY: People won't come to him for –

MISS LANE: All right, Inspector. All right. But just read the letter.

THACKERAY: Which letter?

MISS LANE: There's a letter with the drawings, isn't there?

THACKERAY: (*looking*) There's a type-written page. No name at the bottom. Is that it?

MISS LANE: Yes, that's it. Can I have it for a moment? (*He gives it to her.*) Thank you, Inspector. I'll read it. Just the end of it. Then perhaps you'll understand. (*She reads.*) "I want these drawings back. Please post them this evening to P.O. Box 352, Manchester. I'm not a thief. I don't want any money for this. I just want to stop the sale of this electronic eye. And to stop the sale of any other things like it. Please help me with this. Please. Please . . . . ."